Hamsters: The Complete Hamster Care Guide

How To Make Your Hamster Live For 7 Years Or More

By: Craig Bartley

ISBN-13: 978-1484044209

TABLE OF CONTENTS

Craig Bartley

PUBLISHERS NOTES
BLUE SHIFT PUBLISHING LLC

Disclaimer

This publication is intended to provide helpful and informative material. It is not intended to diagnose, treat, cure, or prevent any health problem or condition, nor is intended to replace the advice of a physician. No action should be taken solely on the contents of this book. Always consult your physician or qualified health-care professional on any matters regarding your health and before adopting any suggestions in this book or drawing inferences from it.

The author and publisher specifically disclaim all responsibility for any liability, loss or risk, personal or otherwise, which is incurred as a consequence, directly or indirectly, from the use or application of any contents of this book.

Any and all product names referenced within this book are the trademarks of their respective owners. None of these owners have sponsored, authorized, endorsed, or approved this book.

Always read all information provided by the manufacturers' product labels before using their products. The author and publisher are not responsible for claims made by manufacturers.

The statements made in this book have not been evaluated by the Food and Drug Administration.

Blue Shift Publishing LLC

7950 NW 53rd Street

Miami,

FL 33166

Craig Bartley

DEDICATION

I want to dedicate this book to my pet hamster Fred. He dies at the ripe old age of 8 and ½ years. I miss his running on the wheel at 3 am. I hope this book makes you have your pet hamster for as long as Fred kept my company.

CHAPTER 1- WHY YOU SHOULD GET A PET HAMSTER

Hamsters can be selected as excellent beginner pets, since they are reasonably easy to care for. These types of pets oftentimes have a tamed disposition and relatively clean practices. Hamsters by nature are friendly and if they are handled often they can become tamed. People are able to find delight in watching these animals go about their daily housekeeping as well as food storing or exercising on their wheel.

A few hamsters will acknowledge the presence of their owners in return for treats when approached, however if they are not handled from very young then they may resent being held and possibly will bite. Docile tempered hamsters that do not have a history of biting may be handled. It is recommended though when handling these kinds of hamsters that you use both hands or in one of your hands you hold the hamster against your body.

Choosing a hamster that has a good temperament is important, as if you should frighten the hamster the possibly exist that you may be bitten by the hamster. Handling these animals gently, taking them up and supporting them in the palms of your hands will help in taming the hamster.

Several hamsters build up treacherous personalities and start biting possibly because they were handled roughly or was abruptly bothered or awakened. When the personality of a hamster is not known then it is important that they are approached with extreme caution. Wearing a pair gloves or wrapping them in little towels to pick them up would be the most appropriate way to handle this kind of pet. In caring for your hamster you can persuade them to go into containers that are Tupperware, since this would allow them to come out of their cage from time to time.

Hamsters that have unknown personalities could be handled by the owner merely taking them up by the skin that is on the back of their neck, as hamsters have a lot of loose skin. Therefore, one would just need to be sure that they hold sufficient skin using their thumb, middle as well as index fingers, as the hamster is still capable of turning completely around and biting the hand of the individual if they are loosely held.

The temperaments of hamsters differ according to the breed and where it is bought. One would say that it is easier to tame golden hamsters and black bears. In several pet stores hamsters are mass produced without thought being given to their health or temperament. It is for this reason why potential hamster owners may want to consider investigating the breed of the hamster or the origins of the pet store hamsters. Hamsters are nocturnal animals; therefore they will sleep during the nights and rust around their cage in the nights. It should be noted that the incisor teeth for hamsters is large and never stop growing.

CHAPTER 2- HAMSTER FACTS: WHAT EVERY HAMSTER OWNER NEEDS TO KNOW

Knowing Your Hamster

The first thing that is noteworthy for hamster owners is that hamsters are night-time rodents. Although a hamster may be in captivity, they will display greater activity at nights rather than during the day. It for this reason why hamsters are reluctant to be handled during the daytime, as their biological clocks are set for them to sleep during the daytime and this in turn allows them to be grumpy and oftentimes bite. Also, hamsters are antisocial by nature and must be kept alone, doing this helps to avoid the fights which could become deadly. Studies have further shown that the only time that hamsters should be put together it is during mating, and even so the readiness of the pet owner to intervene is still needed. The rule is that the female should be place in the male territory. The cage that the hamsters are placed in should be secured as one would want to ensure that the hamsters are not prone to escaping.

Food for Hamsters

The basic food for the hamster should be consisted of lean seeds and not oats; it should be further loaded with carbohydrates and extra fresh plant matter like fruits and vegetables. It is recommended however that bitter fruits and lettuce be avoided. A reasonable amount of powdered minerals and vitamins should be added, it can be scattered over the food in recommended portions. Although the hamster is a rodent the food should still be tailored to the size of the hamster.

Also, pet owners are encouraged to get food that will help with caring for the teeth of their hamsters; single measures ought to be taken as this allows the hamster to get a supply of chewy pieces, which is unprepared wood or chewing biscuits that is sold in pet stores for this particular purpose. Always ensure that your hamster have a supply of fresh water, you can purchase bottles that are specially designed for hamsters. Some hamsters may require that you help them to identify with the bottle and so, you should do this by carefully feeding the hamster with the water from the bottle with the lip as this will help the hamster to make the link between the water and the bottle.

Once the hamster is not provided with a fresh supply of water they may suffer from constipation, having a consistent diet for the hamster and avoid fast changes is very good in developing the right eat practices for your pet. Never feed the hamster with sweets especially chocolate. Avoiding a calcium shortage can be averted once mineral stones are provided for your pet hamster.

Diseases that Affects Hamsters

Hamsters could be stricken by colds that otherwise may affect humans. Therefore, if you have a cold then you should practice proper hygiene likewise if your hamster catches a cold and sneezes as well as its nose begin to run you should clean the cage immediately. Always keep your hamster's cage in a warm area that is free from draught while they have a cold if after a few days the hamster have not recovered from the cold then they should be taken to the veterinarian.

Another common hamster disease is 'English' it is also known as wet tail which is normally accompanied with diarrhea and lethargy. If this disease goes untreated it could lead to the death of your hamster. In order to cure the wet tail, then the pet owner should visit the pet store and purchase the dry tail preparation.

It is important that while your hamster is suffering from the wet tail disease they are given extra liquid to make up for the loss of liquid which resulted from the diarrhea. "Wet tail" could also be as a result of a change in the hamster's environment as well as handling. Hamsters that are young should not be exposed to excessive and sudden handling, as they are very sensitive animals that should not be dropped by an individual that is standing upright.

Syrian Hamster

This breed of hamster goes by other association which regularly mentions the color and fur. This particular breed is the most famous type for pet purposes. A grown hamster can be between ten to fifteen centimeters and must be kept separately except in the case where they are mating.

Chinese hamster

Hamsters of the Chinese breed have tails that are longer than the breeds of hamsters, the body of this hamster is slender and they have a more rat like look. The status of this breed of hamster is not as great as the Russian hamster. The lifespan of the Chinese hamster is approximately two years and this breed may be kept in groups, once they are use to each other from when they were younger.

The Campbells Russian Dwarf Hamster

This dwarf breed of hamster is most appreciated for the purpose of being kept as a pet. An adult in the Campbells Russian Dwarf breed can grow between five to eight centimeters. The Campbells Russian dwarf hamster may be identified by their fur on paws and tail and numerous colours of their fur. Once this particular breed of hamster is introduced to their other hamsters of the same breed from earlier years, then they can be accepting of their racial coounterparts.

Russian Dwarf Winter white Hamster

While very similar to the Campbells Russian breed, the Russian dwarf winter white hamster differs in the sense that although a lot of colours have been bred, this particular hamster changes its fur to white during the winter season and it unable to mate at this time. By means of exception can these hamsters be familiarized to be integrated in groups; however these groups cannot take in other breeds of hamsters.

The Roborovski´s Dwarf Hamster

An adult Roborovski´s dwarf hamster can reach a length of approximately 5 centimeters it is the smallest of all hamster breeds. Its jumpiness and insignificant appearance makes it swift and hard to manage. These hamsters could by way of exception be adapted to living in groups, but they must be familiarized from earlier years. The life span of the Roborovski Dwarf Hamster is around three years.

CHAPTER 3- TYPES OF HAMSTERS: WHICH TYPE IS BEST FOR A PET

Five known kinds of hamsters exist; they are the Campbell's Russian Dwarf Hamster, the Syrian Hamster, Roborovski Hamster, the Chinese Dwarf Hamster and Dwarf White Winter Russian Hamster.

The Syrian Hamster

This particular kind of breed enjoys living alone in the wild as well as in captivity. The Syrian Hamster has the potential to become violent with another hamster of the same breed or otherwise and can inflict serious injure. Therefore it is never advisable that this breed of hamster be kept in pairs. It should be noted however that this breed of hamster is normally found in pet stores.

The Syrian Hamster is also known as the Golden hamster, this is as a result of its unique wild golden color, even though nowadays there are several different colors and coat mutation of hamsters. The 'Fancy Hamster' or 'Standard Hamster' as this breed is also referred to as usually have long hair and a Teddy Bear appearance, the female in this breed is however larger than the male.

The Dwarf Winter White Russian Hamster

The Djungarian Dwarf Hamster also known as the White Winter Russian Dwarf Hamster was discovered in the prairieland of Siberia and Northern Kazakhstan. When this breed of hamster is placed outdoors during the winter it acquires a white looking coat. This white coat is a normal defensive colour that appears while the hamster's environment is cover up in snow. Hamsters are for the most part relaxed at temperatures between 65 ° F / 18° C to 80°F / 26°C and must at all times be kept indoors.

This breed of hamster may be housed in a group setting, if possible of the identical gender. The Djungarian hamsters can only be housed in group settings if they were brought together from a young age.

The Dwarf Campbell's Russian Hamster

Both the Campbell's Russian Dwarf Hamsters and Winter White Russian Dwarf Hamsters are very much related. Due to the fact that the Campbell's coat is thicker they emerge as larger than the Winter White Russian Dwarf Hamster, however this is not factual. Campbell's Hamsters are inclined to grow to be fatter in captivity than the Russian Hamsters. The coat of the Dwarf Campbell's Russian Hamster is yellow-brownish and has a lean, piercingly wizened dorsal stripe. The coat of this hamster turns somewhat greyer in winter. This breed of hamster can cohabit in groups of the exact gender. The length of the Dwarf Campbell's Russian Hamsters is approximately 8-11cm long.

The Roborovski Hamster

The dumpy tailed dwarf hamster known also as the Roborovski Hamster has a yellow-brownish coloring and outstanding whiskers provides this species of hamster with a completely dissimilar appearance to the other two short-tailed kinds of Dwarf Hamsters.

The Roborovski breed of Hamsters are fewer and not always known, they have very few offspring. The Roborovski is the smallest of the Dwarf hamster breed and can measure anywhere between 4 to 5.5cm in length, the tail of this hamster is hardly visible. On the back of the Roborovski Hamster it is brownish-yellow with grey coloring underneath. Occasionally the yellow on the back of this breed of hamster looks rusty in color and they do not have posterior stripes. Roborovski Hamsters could live up to three years and in group settings of the similar gender.

The Chinese Hamster

The Chinese Dwarf Hamster has a long-tail and is not directly related to the other Dwarf Hamsters. The coat of this breed of hamster is not as vague as the other species of hamsters. The fur on the Chinese hamster lays close up and dark-brown posterior stripe is on its back. It is not always obviously detectable and the belly of this hamster is light grey. The ears on the Chinese Hamster are dark and lightly edged. The scrotum of the male is noticeably large.

This particular breed of hamster is of a calm temperament and is with no trouble handled although they appear initially to be a little aggressive, however if you display patience they become tamed. The usual lifetime of a Chinese Hamster is from one and half to two years. These hamsters can grow to as much as 10 to12cm long with the male being bigger than the female.

CHAPTER 4- HAMSTER CAGES: DIFFERENT TYPES OF CAGES AND WHICH ONE IS THE BEST

Purchasing a new cage for your pet hamster is important and there are a variety of cages that one can select from in the pet store. As hamster owners you are not only limited to buying your pet hamster's cage from a pet store but online as well. When selecting hamster cages pet owners commonly make these two mistakes and they should be avoided. They are:

Mistake 1: Purchasing the Incorrect Type Of Cage

An entirely plastic cage is the only wrong kind for a hamster as it does not permit the hamster with sufficient ventilation. Besides, when selecting a hamster cage there are three main choices, firstly, the entirely wire cage, then the plastic cage that have wire bars and thirdly the aquarium. Any of these three cages can be right cage as well as the wrong one for your hamster.

The Plastic with Wire Cage: once you like colors then the plastic cage with wire bars may be the correct choice for you. This kind of cage comes in various colors and you may even find a color that matches with the room in the house that the hamster will be residing into.

However it is not recommended that you choose the plastic cage if you do not patience, as this cage requires time to be assembled. Oftentimes you will find YouTube videos that illustrate people quickly assembling these plastic cages and it makes the process appear very straightforward, however in reality the plastic pieces require being closely fitted together and may break if twisted too firmly. In addition, it should be noted that these cages will require the same patience and time to pull them apart for cleaning; as a result it may take far more work than the other types of cages.

The Wire Cage: this is an easily assembled cage that is lightweight; it further permits your hamster to do lots of climbing. The wire cage might possibly be the correct choice as the sides of the wires makes it simple to join a water bottle as well as exercise wheel, hence your hamster will have much more space to run about inside the cage.

However if you are getting a Dwarf hamster, the wire cage can be a mistake as the wires in the cage may be too far apart and allowing the dwarf hamster easy access to squeeze through and escaping. Furthermore, if the cage is too big, your dwarf hamster could get hurt if it falls from the top of the cage.

Aquarium Cage: if you are the type of owner that enjoys watching your pet then the aquarium cage is an excellent choice since all four sides is made of glass. It is also very hard for your hamster to escape from this type of cage, as it cannot climb up the sides of the glass aquarium cage.

Like any other choice in a cage, the aquarium cage may be the wrong option if you are not able to lift anything heavier than the other two cage types. Therefore, several factors must be considered when choosing the aquarium cage, if you are someone that may experience difficulty in lifting heavy things then this cage is not the best choice since it can become heavier when cleaning and water is added. In addition with the aquarium cage you have to be cautious about placing a screen at the top of the cage and also ensure that this screen remains in place or your hamster could climb on the toys that are placed in the cage or the hamster tube and escape.

Mistake 2: Purchasing the Wrong Size Cage

A hamster in the incorrect sized cage will become extremely unhappy. Therefore hamster owners are encouraged to have a cage that will give them enough space to work out and play. This means that hamster pet owners ought to buy the correct size for the kind of hamster that they have.

Clearly the Goldens, Teddy Bears and Syrians, are bigger than the Russians and Roborovski's dwarf hamsters and would need more room.

The bigger hamsters ought to have a cage that is no less than 10"L by 16"W by 16"H or 25 x 40 x 40 cm. For the cages that are wire, it is recommended that hamster owners get cages that are three storeys which could be 14"L by 11"W by 25"H or 35 x 28 x 63 cm is a good option. The aquarium cages should be a minimum of 10 gallons.

The owners of maybe two dwarves could fit then into smaller cages. Nevertheless, keep in mind that they will more than likely be active roundabout the same time; therefore they will require lots of exercise space.

Irrespective of the mistake that is commonly made hamster owners can make the selection of either the cage space or type still be a problem as it is going to be a problem if we put too much or too little toys for the hamster. If you should place an exercise wheel, bedding, a food bowl, water bottle and toys in a cage that is already small, it could cut back on the actual playing and running room. Therefore, be careful not to make mistake of merely looking at the box size in the pet store. Take into consideration the kind of hamster that you are buying or have and how much things you are going to put inside of the cage, then from that make your decision.

CHAPTER 5- HAMSTER WHEEL: A MUST HAVE FOR EVERY HAMSTER CAGE

Hamsters are born with the innate ability to run. In the wild these animals would journey for miles each night searching for food, while it has been documented that even some pet hamsters have run for up to 8km each night on the wheels they use to exercise.

The Surface Used for Running

The hamster wheel is the most appropriate surface for the hamster as it is solid and not steps. It is also attached to the cage's side or can be free standing with no side supports. Using the usual wire wheel that resembles a ladder wrapped in a circle with side bars for support is not the greatest choice as it could cause injuries to the hamster.

The Noise Levels

The fact that hamsters are nighttime animals, it means that they will be using their wheels mainly at nights, with this you may want to purchase a silent wheel. This is particularly true if you are sharing the room with your pet hamster. Probably you may want to spray a squeaky wheel with some vegetable oil.

Size

There are no definite recommendations for the smallest sizes of exercise wheels for hamsters. Those that are mainly marketed for hamsters are usually right, once the owners keep in mind that the wheels that are smaller are more suitable for the dwarf hamsters and the bigger wheels should be used for the Syrian hamsters like the golden and even the teddy bear hamsters. It may be wise that you get the largest hamster wheels that you possibly can get as a wheel that is too small will be uncomfortable for your hamster; however a bigger wheel should pose no problem at all.

Wheels Alternatives

The balls that are known as the run-about balls that is used for exercising outside of the cage is famous, however given the extent of running that most hamsters enjoy doing, these balls will not provide enough exercise for the hamsters as they are very simple ball, which is a wheel form that propels a car structure and other unique shapes. Nowadays a track system is available for hamster owners to set up for their pet hamster's movement in and around its cage. It is important that hamsters are not left into one of these balls for too long as they can suffer from overheating. Therefore 15 – 20 minutes is sufficient and the hamster ball should never be used near stairs as the possibility exists that the hamsters could tumble down the stairs.

Multipurpose Wheels – For Any Cage Type

The famous Wodent Wheel was approved by the ASPCA; it has an eight inch size that is reasonable for almost all hamsters. This multipurpose wheel is also compact with free standing. The distinctive front is semi-solid along with holes for access that is vulnerable to chewing by the hamster.

The Super Pet Noiseless Spinner is obtainable in different sizes; this six and half inch model may be ideal for hamsters that are dwarf however it could be too little for the bigger Syrian hamsters, nevertheless, there is another size that is a very large 12 inches. This particular wheel utilizes ball bearings for silent operation. Free standing could safely be used or attached to the bars of the cage.

The Comfort Wheel, another type of wheel that can be used for the large hamsters, as a matter of fact it would be quite ideal as it is eight and a half inches in diameter. This type of wheel is also inexpensive and may be used free standing or connected to cage.

The Modular Cage Systems using Specialty Wheels

An expansion of your hamster's modular home is achieved through this kind of wheels, but the same problem that is experienced with the plastic modular cage is experienced by the specialty wheels. Certainly one problem that is experienced using the specialty wheels in the modular cage is the issue of ventilation since it is poorly ventilated the probability exist that the hamster could over heat and also there is the issue of cleaning the cage.

The CritterTrail Snap on Wheel for the Super Pet Hamster is six and three quarters inches wheel that fastens to the side of CritterTrail structure cages along with the Critter Trail Funnel tubes. This is most suitable for the dwarf hamsters since it is extremely small.

The S.A.M. Workout Wheel is well-matched with the S.A.M. cage systems. This particular wheel fastens to the exterior of the cage. It is a minute size wheel that is most suitable for the dwarf hamsters.

The CritterTrail Xtreme Super Pet Wheel is a unique-looking wheel from the CritterTrail that is fastened through a Fun-nel tube.

Craig Bartley

Run-About Balls and Others

These kinds of balls should not be used as a replacement for the hamster cage having wheels in the cage. The free-wheeling run-about must never be used near stairs, not all hamsters care about having the ball, but they should not be left too long in the balls or the hamster could run the risk of overheating.

The usual spherical run-about ball comes in different sizes and the one that is 7 inches is ideal for dwarf hamsters and maybe smaller for the Syrian hamsters, however pet owners of hamsters that are bigger ought to consider the model that is 11.5 inches.

Critter Cruiser is a car designed frame that supports a luminous plastic wheel, and as the hamster runs then the car moves. Some settings permit the cruiser to be used either "free-wheeling" or tracks. Otherwise, it can be set for motionless use. This design comes in various sizes and the small size is most suitable for dwarf hamsters.

Hamtrac this is a nifty system that could be utilized with run about balls or Critter Cruiser, all are sold independently. When the plastic pieces of this model are joined it forms an oval "race" track.

CHAPTER 6- HAMSTER BALL: WHAT EXACTLY IT IS AND WHY ITS IMPORTANT TO HAVE ONE

Birds fly, fishes will swim and without a doubt hamsters run. Hamsters will run several kilometers each night when they are in the wild just to search for food.

In reality, a hamster could develop destructive ways and may become ill if it does not get to run on a regular basis. Therefore having the hamster ball is a great way for a pet hamster to do the physical activity that it needs to do, however as a pet owner you need to understand how the ball is used so that it does not result in any issues. Many pet hamster owners will also highlight the fun that an individual can have just watching the hamster run in the ball.

The greatest thing is that you select a ball in which the hamster can remain contentedly. Those balls that have a 17 cm diameter are found to be more appropriate for hamsters that are dwarf, while Syrian hamsters will require bigger balls that have a 28 cm diameter. These little rodents should not have to bend their backs when they are running in the ball; also this accessory should have sufficient ventilation holes that permit the hamster to breathe properly.

Always watch the hamster when it is playing in the ball and ensure that the ball does not roll near any stairs, also be sure that while the hamster is in the ball there is no other animal in the house that will hunt the hamster. Select a time to let the hamster play with the ball when it is most energetic, seeing that hamster are nocturnal animal, it would probably be best that the evening is selected for this type of activity.

Craig Bartley

Originally, the hamster would be a little puzzled about what it is doing in a ball, it may even become scared but it will become warmed up to this activity if a pattern is set. One is able to tell that the hamster is afraid when it is in the ball by the way that it crouches. Allow you're the hamster to play for ten to fifteen minutes then put it back into its age. Irrespective of the ventilation holes the air in the run-about ball become less breathable after the hamster has been in there playing for fifteen minutes.

The hamster will show obvious sin that it is time to remove it from the ball once the hamster's fur become wrinkled and the animal begins to crouch, then it is time to remove he rodent from the ball. It is important that the hamster's ball is cleaned after each use, this can be done by simply washing it with warm water and vinegar, then allow the ball to dry. It is important that the ball is cleaned because dome hamsters will go in the ball, it should be noted that they can be taught out of such practice.

Getting the hamster in the ball may take some getting used to. But you can get the pet into the ball by placing small portions of food inside the ball. Once the food is inside the ball the hamster should then be placed near the ball and it will go into the ball when it is ready.

Chapter 7- Hamster Toys : What To Get For Your Pet That It Will Love

Chewing Toys for the Hamster

Hamsters enjoy chewing, however as member of the rodent family the teeth of hamster is continuously growing and toys that will permit the growing process as well as keeping the pet hamster's teeth In good condition should be purchased. Wooden Chew toys are perfect selections for hamsters. However not all woods will do well for your hamster and hamster owners are encouraged to keep away from chew toys that are made from evergreen and cedar woods and ensure that the chew toys are free from pesticide and chemical.

Use those items that are specially made for pet hamsters. Several people may want to use branches from their backyard there is nothing wrong with that once it is from a pesticide free fruit tree. Blocks of hardwood or shapes are also great so long as it has never been chemically treated.

Cardboard may be used as a harmless chew toy once it is ink as well as dye free. Even though there is presently little helpful proof on the security of colored cardboard, make a mistake on the side of caution and use only plain cardboard like toilet paper or paper towel rolls. Every chew toys ought to be observed and changed after a significant amount of chewing has taken place.

Climbing and Hiding Toys

Hamsters are known natural climbers as well as burrowers, so giving them toys that will encourage their natural instincts is an ideal way to be sure that they get the best of their playing experience while in there are in their caged home. Pet stores store numerous climbing structures as well as hiding houses or huts which are intended for all sizes of hamsters. Wooden ladders are an excellent climbing choice which may also serve as a chew toy.

Wooden ladders may be found in both the hamsters and bird isles in the pet store, however based on the natural chewing nature of your hamster, pet owners should be prepared to replace these structures as required. It is not recommended that hamster pet owners use organic ropes to build hanging walkways or bridges in the hamster's cage as the possibility exist that the hamster may become entangled in the assembly and suffer injuries.

Tunnels that are made from plastic, as well as tubes, and structures that can be used for hide-away could also be bought at the pet store, however should be watched for wear and tear. Hamsters that are compulsive chewers should be carefully monitored as the tiny pieces of plastic may be dangerous to the hamster if it is swallowed continuously. Keeping your pet hamster safe requires frequent checks on all plastic toys and where excessive chewing is taking place then such a toy should be taken out of the cage.

Digging and Grooming Toys

Burrowing and digging are favourite pastime for hamsters; therefore owners could give their hamsters a deep excavating bowl or dish that is filled with chinchilla dust bath, fine sand as well as soil that is sterilized. The dish should be placed at the base of the hamster's cage clear from the food and water bottle. It is recommended that the dish chosen is large enough for the hamster to burrow in and also to roll in as this helps to keep the hamster's coat in healthy condition. Replace the digging material every week when the cage of the hamster is cleaned.

Irrespective of the toy you select for your hamster ensure that you wipe it down prior to giving it to your hamster or putting it into the hamster's surroundings. Wash-down all plastic wheels, run-abouts, houses, huts, and toys with anti-bacterial soap, rinse thoroughly with warm water, and dry them totally prior to permitting the pet to use the new items.

Ensure that the hamster's cage is not overcrowded with toys and always recall that toys that are deemed safe for adult hamster s may not be so for baby hamsters or those that may be sick or pregnant.

Observing the hamster while it is at may be more fun than watching television or surfing the Internet. Their habits and antics are usually always amusing.

The fact that there are several variations available in the toys for hamsters, then you are better able to choose the most ideal one toy for the hamster, one that will work ideally with the animal's personality. Giving the hamster several opportunities to play safely is certain to bring hours of happiness to both the pet and the owner.

CHAPTER 8- HAMSTER BEDDING : THE BEST BEDDING TO HAVE IN THE CAGE

Purchasing or adopting a pet hamster requires that one gets several other accessories like its bedding, chew toys and others. The bedding for hamsters aids in the protection of these little animal feet from the bottom of the hamster's cage, it also absorbs wetness as well as odor and provide the perfect material for hamsters to nest with.

Numerous types of hamster bedding are available, these include paper bedding, wood shavings or wood chips, and those hamsters bedding made from straw. Whichever type of bedding that you prefer it is all accessible at the pet store or pet owners can make these purchases online.

For a number of years, cedar bedding was the customary choice for hamsters. Nonetheless, in modern years it has become less prevalent for cedar to be the choice hamster bedding amongst pet owners. Studies are starting to show that a few chemicals used in the treatment and processing of wood shavings could impact the hamster's health. Hamsters are inclined to chew the material used for their bedding and may unintentionally swallow the chemicals that are on the material.

It does not mean that owners of hamsters should omit using wood shavings completely. Several soft wood shavings are obtainable that do not have harmful chemicals and therefore is reasonably safe for use as hamster bedding. If wooden shavings are selected as bedding for pet hamsters, then it is encouraged that the pet owner pick wood pulps or pine wood as bedding and it is important that pet owners ensure that the bags are clearly labeled specially for hamsters.

Recycled newspaper that makes hamster bedding or other paper is quickly becoming the choice bedding among hamster owners. This ink-free paper is obtainable either as pellets or shreds, and it makes an outstanding substitute to customary cedar chips as well as shavings. This bed is highly absorbent and free from dust and is the best choice of bedding that is inexpensive and the best choice for the hamster cage.

Common choices such as straw, wheat and other plant fibers are suitable choices for hamster bedding. Several beddings are made with these materials and it is compostable, whereas other forms of this bedding are harmless to flush in the toilet. Therefore, if you reside in an apartment or an urban area, this particular kind of hamster bedding is the best option for these kinds of areas as it is easier to dispose of this type of bedding as you can simply flush it down the toilet.

Once the choice have been made to adopt an animal, it is important that you take responsibility for the care of that animal's health. In caring for a hamster, it is important that research carefully the types of toys, food, accouterments, as well as bedding that are harmless for your new pet.

Converse with the local pet store owners or read online sites that are reputable to make a decision about the type of bedding that will work for your hamster and your living situation. It is suggested that to select a bedding that is most appropriate for your budget and one that will keep the hamster healthy and producing little to no dust as well as easy to be cleaned.

CHAPTER 9- HOW TO CLEAN YOUR HAMSTERS CAGE

It is not impossible for children to learn how to clean the cage of a hamster. When all that is required is readily available it will make the job easier and smoother.

Ensure the hamster is in a play area that is safe and well-contained while cleaning the cage. The hamsters really like to be running around in the exercise balls during the cage cleaning process. If this method is chosen, ensure that the animal is being monitored and the location equipped to contain it if there is an occurrence where the ball opens.

Pull down the cage then clear the bedding. Ensure that the cage cleaner wears a pair of gloves. There are hamster cages that are made to allow the top to pull away from the tray at the bottom. Others are somewhat harder to difficult. There is a type of hamster cage which completely comes apart to make cleaning easier. If this is the kind of cage that the hamster is living in, it is not recommended that children clean it. Teach the children the art of scooping out and throwing away the bedding that is soiled. A scoop for cat litter is handy in this process. Hamsters love to store food but it can get stale. Clean out the stored food.

Get the cage and the accessories washed. Ensure that the tray at the bottom is cleaned thoroughly and also the cage bars and sides. The food dish should be cleaned also with a mild soap. Cleansing solutions for cages are sold at stores that provide pet supplies. A dish soap that is environmentally friendly, chemical-free, and free of fragrances and dyes is recommended. It would be a good thing not to allow soap to touch the mouth of the hamster.

Reassemble the cage of the hamster and put back the bedding. The hamster cage design will determine the ease of placing the toys and bedding into the tray at the bottom prior to placing the remainder of the cage together again. Let the children look what you are doing and practice to do it properly.

CHAPTER 10- WHAT TO FEED YOUR HAMSTER

If hamsters are given a nutritional and balanced diet they will be at a healthy level. For hamsters, the most ideal method for keeping them healthy is to buy the commercial brand of hamster food. This will ensure balanced nutrition and it will appeal to the palette of the hamster. In addition, it must be emphasized that the hamster get fresh and constant water supply.

It is most ideal to have a water bottle which attaches to the hamster's cage. If there is no convenience for a water bottle at the side of the cage, a bowl is just as good. It is required that a heavy bowl is chosen so that it cannot be tipped over easily. The water supply will be required to be refreshed every day and that the water is also not stagnated and contaminated.

The diet of the hamster can be supplemented with added vegetables and fresh fruits every now and again. Fresh food is really not a requirement for adequately balanced food mix for the hamster but the hamster may like the idea of the different foods in the diet. In addition, the time that is used to feed the hamster with a treat can be utilized as interaction time with the pet hamster.

There are some foods that should not be fed to the hamster because they can result in digestive or health issues or can be poisonous and/or toxic to the hamster:

Ensure that the hamster do not eat almonds, cabbage, apple, seeds, citrus fruits (lemon, tangerine, orange, grapefruit, and others), garlic, eggplant, red or kidney beans, mushrooms, rhubarb, onion, pickles, junk food that humans eat like chips, chocolate and others.

What Will the Hamster Find Enjoyable?

Nuts and Seeds: Hamsters normally like seeds and nuts. These are great treats and are usually included in several commercial pet foods. Make sure that they are not too many seeds or nuts to a hamster of the dwarf family. These types of foods have a high level of fat and may result in a situation called 'heat' in the dwarf hamster. This can cause them to lose fur. It is fine to give one to two nuts every two days to a dwarf hamster.

Green Vegetables: One other wonderful treat for hamster is green vegetables. They will appreciate a little slice of cucumber (great water source) or lettuce every now and again. Be careful that it is not overdone. This should not be fed to them for more than one time every two to three days. Too much lettuce can result in liver issues for the hamster so this treat should be fed sparingly.

Stay away from sticky treats: Honey and peanut butter are lovely treats for humans but their stickiness can cause the hamster's cheek pouch to become trapped. Generally, sticky foods should not be fed to them as the pouch lining can be affected. Only a veterinarian can fix the problem if the hamster's cheek pouch is impacted because of eating a sticky treat.

When the hamsters are given excessive amount of treats too frequently, gastritis, liver problems and diarrhea can be the result. Foods should be given to the hamsters in moderation and in room temperature.

Some Foods Approved for Hamster (some of these are not suitable for dwarf hamsters):

Alfalfa, banana, apple (without seeds), cantaloupe, broccoli, celery, cheerios, cashews, cherries, chestnuts, cauliflower, crickets, cheese, corn, dandelion leaves, cucumber, grapes (skinless), green beans, mango, mealworms, peach, pistachios, peanuts, pumpkin, raisins, raspberries, hay, peas, pear, raspberry leaves, strawberries, spinach, sunflower seeds, turnip, chestnuts, walnuts, zucchini yam.

Ensure that vegetable or fruit pit is removed before giving them to the hamster as they can cause problems if the hamster tries to chew or ingest them. There should be no sugar, salt, spices or oil added.

There are other foods that the hamster can be fed. This list is not comprehensive. These are only the common foods that the hamster can eat.

CHAPTER 11- CHECKING ON THE HEALTH OF YOUR HAMSTER

Hamsters may be quite robust pets yet their smallness cause illness and injuries to become serious quickly. If any symptoms of illness is noticed in the hamster, it is required that a veterinarian be consulted as soon as possible. The signs include inactivity, crouching in the corner, appetite loss, untidy or ruffled coat, wheezing, eye or nose discharge, diarrhea and wetness in the tail area. The loss of hair may be a sign that parasites or skin disease is present and also calls for a visit to the veterinarian.

Whenever the hamster is injured or ill, it should be kept warm and urged to eat even a little bit of food as well as water. If necessary, use a dropper to accomplish this until the animal is able to see a vet.

Respiratory Infections: Hamsters are likely to infections that relate to the respiratory which can result in pneumonia. Nose or eye discharge as well as sneezing are signs of an infection. Labored breathing and wheezing are also signs. There is no real need to worry about occasional sneezing but if it is accompanied by reduced activity, appetite loss, difficulty in breathing and wheezing, a vet should be seen right away.

Abscesses: These may be formed from relatively minor skin breaks and are infection pockets. Pus gathers and stores under the skin to form a noticeable lump. This sometimes drains without prompting. Abscesses may come about from scratches or cut found on the skin as well as in cheek pouches if food material that is abrasive manages to scratch the pouches inside lining. If a hamster appears to continuously have food stuffed in the cheeks, there might be an impacted cheek pouch or abscess present. A veterinarian will need to drain, flush and treat the abscess with antibiotics.

Diarrhea: There are several infections that can trigger diarrhea. This can include but is not limited to the wet tail condition. Diarrhea from diet changes as well as antibiotics treatment is also possible. When the hamster gets excessive amounts of fresh foods such as vegetables, this can also cause diarrhea. When this happens, there is no appetite loss of reduction in activity.

A genuine concern is dehydration therefore it should be ensured that the hamster is having water to drink if there is an occurrence of diarrhea. A vet should also be consulted. Also, fresh foods should be withheld for a little while and should only be resumed if there is total resolution of the diarrhea issue. Following this, fresh foods should be slowly reintroduced.

Wet Tail: This condition is also known as regional enteritis and proliferative ileitis. This disease is highly contagious and is more often found in hamsters that have been weaned recently. Although the root of it is not certain, it is believed that Campylobacter jejuni bacteria might be involved. It is believed also that in some instances, there may be diet changes, crowding or stress may be associated with it.

Any hamster that is affected can die quite quickly and show signs like lethargy, appetite loss, diarrhea (resulting in wetness in the tail area), and unkempt coat. However, not every diarrhea occurrence is a sign that the disease is present.

CHAPTER 12- WHAT TO DO IF YOUR HAMSTER ESCAPES

There are ways to find out where the hamster is hiding if it should escape.

If it is not certain which room the hamster is dodging in, put some seeds of sunflower in each of the rooms. Take note of how many seeds were left. Do this before going to sleep. If some seeds are noticed missing in the morning, it will be known exactly which one of the rooms the hamster is hiding.

Place some food in its cage and let the cage remain open and put somewhere that the hamster is suspected to be hiding. The rodent may want to return to the cage by night time.

A hamster trap can also be used. Design a slope (wood plank for instance) leading to a bucket which has food in it. Ensure that food is trailing from the floor, up the slope, to the bucket. The hamster will follow it and more likely will jump in the bucket to get the food that is there. Ensure that the bucket sides are adequately high to prevent it from escaping again. Butter is ideal to be placed on the sides.

Another method is leaving some hamster mix or any other treat on the ground. Place a flour circle around this heap. The hamster will probably not be able to resist this gift. It will then be discovered because of the white and tiny paw prints.

It is also effective to turn everything that makes a noise off like the fan, radio and TV and stand up unmoving. The hamster will be heard shuffling around after a little while.

CHAPTER 13- TAKING YOUR HAMSTER ON THE ROAD : WHAT TO DO

To make sure that the hamster's experience in travel is great, remember the security items that should be included with the other accessories and baggage. Store the bedding and regular food and also a travel cage that is comfortable if it is not possible to bring the regular cage. If life is kept as standard as possible by giving familiar objects, there will be less stress for the hamster.

Carrier

The item that is considered most essential when travelling with a hamster is a carrier that is escape-proof and well-built. The plastic type would be most ideal.

It is not every airline that allows the hamster to accompany the traveler as a pet to carry in the compartment for passenger. Ensure that a check is made with agent doing the booking.

Carriers that have all-wire construction should be avoided when travelling as well as the ones that are created from cardboard. The required seclusion is not provided by these carriers and they are not designed to be used for long periods. They are not suitable to be used for airline travelling.

Make sure that a label is attached to the carrier having the name of the hamster, owner, vet and telephone numbers and addresses for place of residence as well as the destination point.

Water and Food

Allow the hamster to remain on its regular diet. Pack to carry enough food that is familiar as well as treats. If it is not certain that the brand of food that is fed to the hamster will be available at the destination, then enough should be packed to serve for the length of the trip. Take bottled water also.

Medications and Emergency Kit To Bring

Carry all medications that will be required and which were prescribed by the veterinarian of the hamster. Pack cotton balls and swabs as well as mineral oil for cleaning up the ear and eyes. It is always a good idea to carry along a small amount of suitable tick or flea spray or powder.

CHAPTER 14- HAMSTER BREEDING : A COMPLETE GUIDE

If you are interested in learning the process of breeding you can learn some things below.

Breeding hamsters

Hamsters are generally bred according to the specific breed; that is, breeding solely Chinese hamsters or Syrian hamsters. It is not suggested that hamsters are bred of varying breed types. If a friend owns a hamster that is of similar breed and of the opposite sex, arrangement can be made to breed the hamsters. Both owners can now share the problem of finding homes for young hamsters.

What is the most ideal age to begin breading hamsters?

For the female hamsters, the best age to begin breeding is when they are 4 to 6 months. Any age that is younger would place the hamster at risk for having a litter that is poor as she still growing herself. This also increases the possibility of cannibalism. If this process is delayed to long, like over 6 months, there is the likelihood of complications at birth. Although male hamsters become sexually active at the young age of 6 weeks sometimes, it is more ideal to wait until they reach 2 to 3 months in age before considering using them to breed. When dwarf hamsters are kept together, 2-3 months in age is their period to start breeding.

How frequent can female hamsters be bred?

Although it is possible to breed the hamster one litter after another, this usually shortens the lifespan of the hamster. It is more ideal to wait until three or four months before breeding the female hamster again. This should allow the body to 'heal' and make her better able to mate when the time comes around. If the regime is kept, the owner is maybe able to get two healthy litters out of a breeding hamster because they generally get sterile around the age of fourteen months. It is possible to get three litters from a breeding hamster, but this is an exceptional occurrence.

Breeding Syrian hamsters

Syrian hamsters usually are held in isolation so owners generally have to be match makers when it is time to breed them. The 'season' for the female hamsters comes around every four days; that is, ovulation takes place at that time. It should be noted that it is only at that time they will be interested in the male hamsters' advances. Fighting will be the result if it is done outside of ovulation time.

How to know when female hamster is in 'season'

Since the hamsters ovulate every four days, if a date was miscalculated, there is the chance of getting it right the next time. The ovulating hamster usually emits an odor described as being musky just prior to coming into season. In addition, it is generally in the evening that the season begins and will go on for a minimum of four hours to a maximum of eighteen hours.

When the season is finished, there is an excretion from the vagina of a mucous discharge that is white and thick. Hamster breeders that are less experienced will take this as the starting point; three more days should be counted following that then an attempt can be made for breeding.

What is to be done following the mating?

Both of the hamsters should be returned to their original cages. The female hamsters will require additional food that the usual during this period of pregnancy. It is ideal to add foods that are rich in protein such as boiled egg, wheat germ (helps in birthing), and tofu. Although she can be handled, it is suggested that the hamster be left alone when it comes closer to the time of birth. On the fourteenth day, clean the cage and remove the exercise wheel. Give the hamster additional nesting material like paper that has been shredded. Then place the cage in a quiet and warm spot and ensure there are no noise and a minimum of disturbance. The only thing left to do is to wait.

What to do when the young hamsters are born?

Allow the hamster to breastfeed the babies up to about three weeks. Ensure that the nest is not disturbed in the time period because she might react by turning on the babies and eating them. There will certainly be strong odor coming from the cage during the period but this is unavoidable and not attempts should be made regarding changing the material for bedding. It is best to simply ignore it for the time being and tolerate the smell. It should be noted though, that even though they are left alone, sometimes they still eat the young. This mostly occurs with the female hamsters that are allowed to breed when they are less than four months old.

Older hamsters will get rid of some of the babies to cut down on the amount of babies. Continue giving the foods with high protein during this period; milk-soaked bread is another idea. In approximately 3 ½ weeks, the newborn hamsters can be weaned and sexed.

CHAPTER 15- CARING FOR A PREGNANT HAMSTER

Pregnancies for female hamsters generally go up to 17 days for the Syrian hamsters and 18-22 days for dwarf hamsters. Not all times will it be easy to discover that the hamster is pregnant, but appearance and behavior changes can give hints that relates to the state of the hamster. Signs include the gathering of bedding to make a nest, more drinking and eating as well as weight gain.

Taking care of the hamster litter

Things that will be required:

Hamster enclosure that is separate

New bedding

Protein-rich foods – oats, cooked chicken, peanut butter, cheese

Take away from the pregnant hamster any other hamster that might be in the cage.

Place the cage with the pregnant hamster in a room that has low traffic and is quiet.

Change the bedding of the cage in the early stage of pregnancy.

Start giving the protein-rich foods to the hamster; ensure she is not overfed.

Visit the cage only to give her water and food and eliminate all stress

If there is any dead young ones noticed following the birth, remove it without touching any of the living pups.

CHAPTER 16- CARING FOR NEWLY BORN HAMSTERS

Following the birth of hamster pups, it should be importantly noted that the mother as well as the babies should be undisturbed for no less than two-three weeks. This will prevent the babies from being harmed as well as the mother not identifying the scent of the babies, resulting in her eating or abandoning her newborns. This is the reason why it is emphasized that the cage should be kept clean during the pregnancy of the hamster.

Making any attempts to clean the cage when the babies are born and up to two weeks can result in undue stress on the family of hamsters. The male hamster should be taken from the cage also when it nears the time of birth as male hamsters have no maternal instinct and can cause the newborn hamsters to experience harm or stress.

It should be noted that there is not much work to do to care for the newborn hamster pups as the mother is capable of doing all the work that is necessary for the healthy development of her babies. The only thing the owner should do is give them a place that is safe for them and adequate type and amount of water and food supply for the family.

ABOUT THE AUTHOR

Craig Bartley grew up on a farm and has always loved animals in general and smaller animals in particular. He has greatly benefited from having hamsters as pets over the years and now his own children have carried on the tradition of making hamsters a part of their household.

Bartley's deep interest in the animals has greatly influenced his decision to study the difference between the various breeds, mass production of the pets, the types of foods that are most suitable, the different types of cages that are available, the diseases by which they are affected and how to guard against these illnesses.